Mosaic Heart - Longing

MJ Sexton

BookLeaf
Publishing

India | USA | UK

Mosaic Heart - Longing © 2023 MJ Sexton

All rights reserved.

Presentation by *BookLeaf Publishing*

Web: www.bookleafpub.com

E-mail: info@bookleafpub.com

ISBN: 9789358316025

First edition 2023

DEDICATION

To my muse Marc,

Thank you for being the absolute BBFWOB a woman could have. Your support, openness, love, and friendship have inspired me in ways I can't even begin to describe. You gave me the courage to be my authentic self always and I will be forever grateful. LUMU

ACKNOWLEDGEMENT

Much is to be said for the unconditional love of family and your closest friends.

This book would not have been made possible without the never-ending love and support of my wonderful husband Wayne, whose constant belief in my dreams and love of all things "me" always lights my path, and the support, love and encouragement of my beautiful daughters, Maddison, and Cassidy. As a family, along with my grandsons Max, Noah, and son-in-law Philip, we are simply the best, and you are my life and love.

My best friends, Raelene, Janine, Loretta, Niki, Hayley & Tracey are my soul sisters and the biggest and best cheerleaders and support a woman could ask for. Our conversations, life stories, love, laughter, and adventures are why this book came to fruition, and I will forever love you all and feel blessed in every way for having you in my life.

Thank you everyone. You will remain forever in my heart, and I love you.

PREFACE

I have spent my life observing how people interact with each other and how we all want to be loved. After many discussions with people from all walks of life, my own personal experiences, and the common issues I see in my practice as a counsellor, I have concluded that there are basically four stages to a relationship: longing, lust, love, and loss.

Each stage can be experienced on its own or in conjunction with any of the others. Sometimes, we may enter one stage, such as longing for example, and not progress further. Usually, we experience the whole gamut in a relationship, and each term may represent something different to each individual.

In my first book, *Mosaic Heart*, I have focused mainly on the first stage, longing, and have listened, observed, and interpreted through poems how this can affect our thoughts and ideas on what we want and need out of a relationship and our innate desire to be loved and longed for in return.

LAID MY SOUL BARE

I look back at all my words to you
The thousands and thousands of words
I have written over the years
No one has a better insight
Into the way my mind works
Than you.
I have held nothing back,
Laid my soul bare
Burst my heart wide open.
I wear a dozen hats
Friend, lover, mother, sister, child
I support you
Uplift you
Tell it the way I see it
Accept you exactly as you are
But more importantly
Love you unconditionally,
Probably more,
Than anyone else in this world.
My words are my bridge

To you,
To a world of magic
Hope and possibility
Of calm and dreams fulfilled
Of desires met
Of adventure
Laughter
Lust
And love
Deep, deep eternal love
That these mere words
Will never do justice to.

HOW LOST WE ARE

It's easy to drift away
Lost in dreams of what might be
I see you so clearly
And even in silence
The comfort between us
Wraps around me like a warm thick cloak
We laugh at the same things
Our sense of humour
Just slightly twisted
Our eyebrows raise in unison
At strange nuances only we see
No one would ever guess
At how lost we are
Wishing
Wanting
Hoping
For the dreams to become real
And we entwine
In body, in soul
As well as the mind.

DREAMS

I dream with the hopes
I will see you, and feel you
next to me.

Your face appears beside mine,
you kiss my lips tenderly.

Your arms enfold me into you,
warmth invades my body, whole.

Your words, your touch, your essence,
takes over my mind and soul.

If this is what I already feel, within
the depths of just my dreams.

It would only make sense that
in reality, it would be even better than that,
it seems.

I awoke with the waves subsiding,
orgasmic pleasure coursing through
my veins.

My body responds to the longing of whispers,
the thoughts, the dreams, and
the memory of your name.

Only time will tell if this remains a dream
or if reality will come to pass.

But for now, let me return to dreaming,
where all those thoughts, can take flight.

This has become my favourite reverie,
every single night.

PART OF YOUR WORLD

There is nothing quite like that feeling,
when two people discover,
each other,
for the first time.

The rush of excitement, nervousness,
awe,
blended into a molten mix of pleasure
that runs through our veins.

A first kiss,
a first touch,
then the sensual,
magical awakening,
when bodies melt into each other.

For whatever length of time,
that person becomes, a part of your world.

For some,
it will be the last of their firsts.
For others,
the first of many.

Some chase that feeling endlessly
throughout their lives,
while,
others reignite it,
every time they look into the eyes,
of the one they choose.

As the years fly past,
hair turns to grey,
bodies sag and fail,
one touch,
one kiss,
one look,
the knowing,
that they are there for you,
makes all the difference in a life,
well lived.

For we have loved and
been loved in return.

FIRSTS

There is nothing quite like that feeling,
when two people discover,
each other,
for the first time.

I want to see the world
Through your eyes
With the wonder of a child.

I want to breathe the air
Through your mouth
Like the first breath of a newborn.

I want to touch
Through your fingers
Like a toddler playing in the sand.

I want to hear
Through your ears
Like a baby first hearing its mother's voice.

I want to taste
With your tongue
Like an infant first tasting food.

I want to feel
Through your heart
The unconditional love between a mother and
her child

I want to experience it all
Fresh and new
All the firsts in life
Through you
In you
With you

HOW IS THAT SO

How do you miss someone
who has only been around for a little while?
How do you feel so close
when it is still so new,
and each day is just an exploration beneath the
layers you see?
How do you have the same thoughts and ideas
as someone you have just met?
How can they make you smile and laugh so
easily?
How have they got under your skin so fast?
Is this fate, kismet, serendipity?
Were they sent to you for a reason?
You thought your life was pretty good,
then they came along, and
now it's even better.
How is that so?

LIVES ENTWINED

I look forward to tell you everything
And cherish what you think
Your opinion and ideas
Mean more to me
Than all that I have known

Yet choices keep us separate
Distance we enforce
Protect us from disapproving eyes
Of societal discourse

Except for the words I send
That form each heartfelt text
Messages quick and simple
A quote,
Or maybe an emoji or two
Is just my way
Of letting you know
How often I think of you

In the perfect world
Of my dreams
And fantasies combined
You are the one
That I choose
We live our lives entwined

JUST FOR YOU

See through the layers
To all that I am
Do not be afraid to touch me
For I will not break

Listen to my words,
Hear my heart punctuate each,
For they glide through my pen like honey
Dripping with my longing,
The need for you to know me
Better than anyone ever has

I am real
Hiding behind self-built
Walls of stone
And parchment paper
Peaking through cracks
Watching you,
Hoping you spy on me too

You can feel me.
I see it in your face.
You know I am here,
On the other side of this page

Your eyes trail across letters,
That form the words I need to say
But my voice cannot sound
For fear of a stutter or
Unintelligent jumbled mess

So, I reach inside of you,
In the only way I know how
With words for you only
I plant the deepest soul kiss
That only poets know is true.

My heart speaks to yours,
In a love language
All of our own

I call your name in whispers.
A secret wish,
Carried on timeless winds
That swirl around you
As a gentle reminder
That somewhere I exist

Knowing that when you really,
Allow yourself to hear
Allow yourself to feel
Allow yourself to see
You will understand the truth

That I have been right here
All along,
Waiting,
Just for you.

DEEP DESIRE

There is a deep desire
To make you whole
To make you feel
Like nothing before
To take you to a place
Where time doesn't exist
To bring you to
The beyond of bliss
I'd caress your body
Every inch with care
Embed it in my memory
For when you're not there
Trace each line
Every curve, every dip
With my fingers,
With my tongue
With the softness of my lips
I'd trace the lines
Of laughter on your face
Feather the hairs of your brow
With the tips of my nail
Discover every freckle
Each mole and scar
Kiss them gently
Outline them in a star
I'd lay my head

Listen to your heart, beat
Match each breath to yours
Wrap my arms around your waist
Mimic each sigh and moan
As I savour your unique taste
An hour could go by
A day, a month, a year or two
I could have my fill
Yet still not get
Enough of you

BEFORE THE LIGHT OF DAY

You come to me at night
Stealing the bed covers
Sliding in behind me
Curling your body around mine
Brushing the hair from my sleep-laden face
Fitting so perfectly into curves of space

I feel your breath as you kiss my cheek
Your arm snaking around me
Pulling me close
Your fingers begin to wander
Leaving sparks of aliveness on my skin
This is the way we always begin

I flutter between the state of dream and awake
My body responds to your touch
My eyes remain closed but
I want you so much

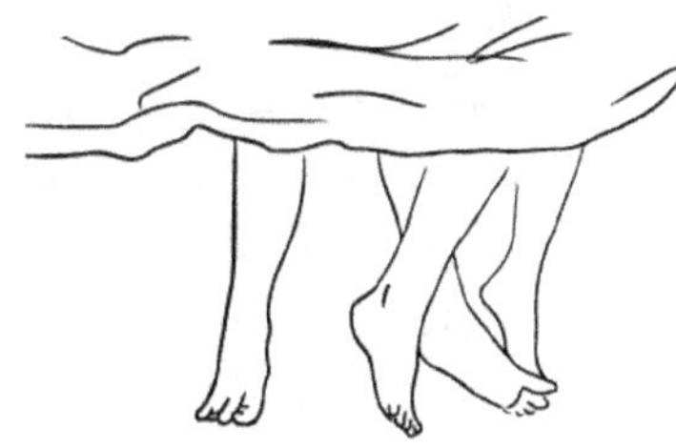

Your hand cups the curve of my full breast
You trail kisses across my bare shoulders
Your fingers encircle, tweaking my nipples taut
A soft moan escapes my lips
I feel your hardness as you rock your hips
My back sways, angling my body forward,
With no further prep
You slide into my softness
No holds barred
I am wet and ready
You are rock-hard

Our tempo is steady
Slow and deep
We have all night
No need for sleep

We stop and start
Going to the edge and back
Revelling in the slowness
The closeness
The feel of being just one

For hours we play
Turning this way and that
Knowing soon we would freefall
Before the light of day
Peaks through the gap
Between curtains and wall

You move right, I move left
You pivot, I twist
You rise, I grind
Our slow dance of ecstasy
Doesn't miss a beat, it
Makes us lose our mind

Words whispered
Breath quickened
Long sighs
The crescendo builds
The tempo pulses
The tide turns
A wave crashes
We ride it together
Landing safely on the shore
Together apart
Two bodies once more

The alarm shrills loudly
Shocking my brain awake
I reach for you
But you're not there
Disappointment sours my body's bliss
Surely a dream can't feel like this

Ecstatic and real
Your touch branded my skin
I opened my soul and let you in

A thin line between
What should be and is true
The truth is...
My soul and body belong to you.

JUST FOR FUN

My thoughts about you change from day to day
I cannot see your face
But I hear what you say
Your words take me to realms
I'd never dared to venture
Inspired, indulgent, passionate
I surrender
To the way you call to me
Sight unseen
You are the type of lover
Of which one can only dream
To have and to hold
Is no longer the goal
I want your words
So sexy and bold
They embrace that place deep within me
Make me believe all the things
That you say but can't see
I am a Goddess, turning 85 this July
My God, are you really 25 and so fly

There is no wall when true love abounds
And age doesn't matter when you have
What we've found in one another
This match is made in heaven
I will meet you online precisely at seven
Where we can slip away and
Just be ourselves
Into our longings and imagination, we delve
Away from judgment and prying eyes
Our words of love travel through the skies
Via cables and networks, and internet guides
To the place where we both beat as one
Chatroom 7692
Just for Fun

TOO MUCH

I say too much
I say not enough
I bear my soul
Put my heart on the line
But the words get lost in translation

I feel too much
I want too much
I care too much
And yet it is all I have

I am one click away from madness
One text away from defeat
I am the ghost in your corner
No face, hands, or feet

I am only words on a screen
No body, a meme
With a heart that beats strong
Pounds the letters of your name
You are alive in every part of me
You reside inside my brain

How is it that we got this way
You so real and I, not
Why does it hurt so much

When you sign off
And leave me behind
Stuck somewhere in between cyberspace
And the dark places in my mind

When do I matter and become real?
When will what I feel,
Matter?

HUNGER

There's a hunger for you
One I find hard to even describe
I long to feel you skin-to-skin
Break down the barriers
Behind which we hide

Lay behind me
Fill the curves of my spine
Mesh your body into me
Feel the fire between our lines

I want to memorise
Every inch of you
Store it safely away
So that the days we are often apart
I can recall it all to play

I need to smell the scent of you
In deep breaths
That fill my lungs
And attach it to my memory fibres
For the days I'm all alone

Alight the sense on my tongue
With the taste of you
So sweet

A meal would never again taste as good
Once I've had you as a treat

Let me feast my eyes on you
From every angle, I'd take a view
Place it in my memory movie vault
Play it like breaking news

Crawl deep inside of me
Melt into me now
Become one, our bodies entwined
Satiate my hunger
As only you know how

I could probably have my fill
Yet it would still
Not be enough
The taste, the sight, the scent of you
Makes me crave you even more

It is your mere touch
Your very presence
The essence, that is only you
Is what I hunger for.

INVISIBLE STRINGS

It's in the moments when I'm alone
That I think of you the most.
A song on the radio, a sign, a colour
All remind me of you.
The tears fill my eyes,
And burn behind my lids.
They are not of sadness but
Opportunities missed.
The choices we make,
All reflect where we are now.
Are you happy with what you decided?
I can't answer that without a sigh.
For I know our souls collided,
Changing me for the better,
Expanding all my senses,
Making me think more outside of myself,
Looking at the World through different eyes,
Seeing what really makes me happy,
Watching you fly.

There are invisible strings that bind us,
Strengthened by an undeniable love.
I've never known anyone like you,
A beautiful bird that needs to be free,
But longs for the gilded cage
Of belonging, acceptance, and responsibility.
You don't draw attention to yourself,
Yet those who meet you fall under your spell.
They know you are different
A little just left, of the norm.
I see you for all that you are,
Inside, the place you hide,
The recesses of your mind.
The things you desire.
Your secrets are safe with me,
I honour all of you.
My tears now flow freely
For we are but one, not two.
I would lay at your feet,
If it meant that you could rise.
I am a pillar in your life,
An invisible support.
Near or far,
I am always by your side.
Opportunities missed need to be revised
Our lives are not over,
Really just begun.
Wherever we go,
Together or apart,

We will always be,
Not two, but as one.

THESE WORDS

I don't have to always see you,
Or feel your skin next to mine.
You are so ingrained in my being,
Growing stronger with time.

I see you,
Your face,
Your smile,
Your eyes,
The mismatch of skin colour where,
Your neck and shoulder meet.
It is my favourite spot,
To nestle my head,
Whenever we hug to greet.

It's from here I memorised your scent,
Fresh as a summer breeze,
After the evening rain.
It floods my senses,
Revitalises my brain.

I hear you,
Your laugh echoes through my mind,
It brings a smile to my face.
Your voice,
Its own sweet cadence is
So easy to trace.

I feel you,
Your heart beats through me,
In a tune all of its own.
It makes my heart skip a beat,
In the moments I am alone.

I need you,
As much as the air I breathe.

Without you,
My life would have no meaning, it
Would lack in all its joy.

I look to you,
To inspire me,
In everything I do.

I love you,
Unconditionally.
These words,
Are my proof.

PARALLEL EXISTENCE

We are busy, you and I
Living lives in a parallel existence
Distanced by time and circumstance
At the end of the day,
You go your way,
I go mine
But I never turn off.

You are as close to me
As if you were right here
You live inside of me,
I consider you in everything,
In every thought and idea, I have.

The only thing that gets me through
When I can't see or hug you
And believe me, I want to, so bad,
Is the most profound love I have
And the space that I hold for you only.

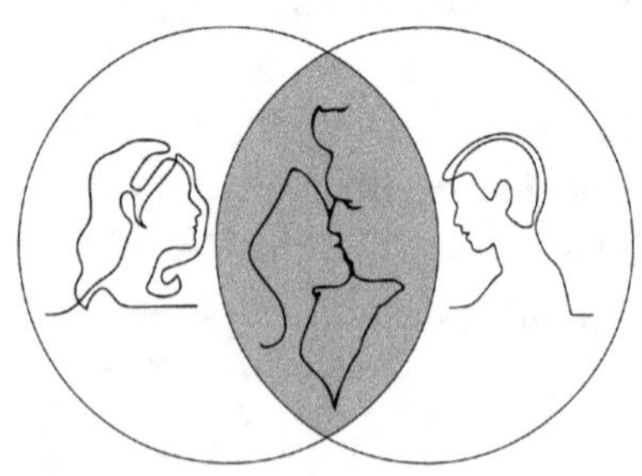

It makes me sad,
That I can't massage away your tension,
From a day gone awry,
Offer you a drink
Or cook you a nourishing meal
To calm you from the inside.
I'd sit and listen as you unload your day
Wrap my arms around you,
Hold you tight
Reassure you that you did the best you could
To make everything all right

It hurts
That I can't share the things
That make up everyday life, because,
You go home to someone else
And I,
I am someone else's wife.

CRUEL REALITY

I woke up this morning
Disappointed I was alone
I swear your scent is
Still on my skin

In my dreams again
Our bodies danced in sync
Making love in fluid waves
As night became day

Your touch was my touch
We mirrored each other
Knowing exactly the steps
Of our dance

We moved around the bed
In time together, to
The music of our heartbeats,
Our own special song

I can still feel your lips
The weight of your hands
As they played my body,
Like the maestro you are

In cruel reality
We are not lovers,
Barely even friends.
Yet my soul tells me
That we should be.

YET

I trust You
I fear You
I love You
I free You
I want You
I need You
I see You
I feel You
I touch You
I hear You
I taste You
I dream You
I breathe You
I respect You
I take You
I tease You
I taunt You
I confuse You
I encourage You
I support You
I and You
Strong alone
Strengthened together
Yet still apart
The torment of
My beating heart.

TRUE DESIRES

I'd fuck you into eternity
Given half the chance
I'll make your body swing and sway
In our cosmic dance

We'd do things never done before
Taking the other
To new heights,
Exploring undiscovered territory
Encouraging each to soar.

It would not just be a body thing
But a joining of the mind
The part that's always locked away
The bit we leave behind

Trying to be normal
Trying to fit in
Putting aside our true desires
Believing they're a sin

It's ok to want a little more
Explore the dark side too
The voyeuristic, the kinky,
Things that are taboo
People often misunderstand

The calling of their soul
It does not make them weird or bad
That longing takes its toll

Wanting something outside ourselves
Searching for a perfect fit
Who would embrace us unconditionally
Allow us to submit

Let's play together in our fantasies
Eyes open wide
Exploring the depths of sexuality
Taking it all in our stride
No judgement
No disgust
Pleasure only
Insatiable lust

So, take my hand
And you can lead, or
I will be your guide
Let's take this ecstatic journey
Together, side by side.

YOU ARE THE SUN

How many times have I felt this heat
That makes me question all I believe
Why is it so easy to fall head-long
Into galaxies, I may not ever belong
Why do I want you in the way that I do
It makes no sense to me or you
I don't question if you feel the same
Afraid to hear "no" to feel the shame
Of not being enough
Not worthy of you
We come from different worlds, fairytale and
real
I can't ever imagine I would hold any appeal
For I look at you
Think you could hold the world in your hand
And I am not larger than life
In the way you are
Your essence, your light
Is brighter than any star
You are the Sun
The centre of my world

It is around you that I sway and swirl
You make me unsteady
Unsure of myself
I never know if you truly understand
Everything that I feel, for all the things I stand
For the belief I have, in the power of you
It is the strongest thing I have ever felt
It is unconditional
It is true
The one I adore the most
Will always be you.

TO BE

To be wanted
To be loved
To be cherished
To be held
To be desired
Unleashes passion
Usually withheld
Because doubt
Makes us question
All we are worth
Where do we fit
In this life here on Earth
Then, one special person
Enters our realm
Fills our hearts
And our minds
Weaves a spell
Full of magic
And of hope
Future dreams
Deep, lasting love
Sets us on a path
Adventures unknown
But in reality
Lead us home
To the place

We belong
With the ones
We adore
To the people
We'll love
Forevermore

WHERE YOU BELONG

Sleep eludes me once again
My body craves you
My mind's in a spin

I long for your touch
The taste of your skin
Tongues dancing together
Sweat mixed with desire
The scent of our sex
Hanging thick in the air

If I imagine hard enough
I can feel you move inside
With each deep stroke
We reach the high
It peaks in a rush
From the core of us both
Muscles clenched then twitch
Ebb then pulse
Milking love's liquid
In spurts which flow
Drench my quivering thighs
Soak the sheets below

Hearts racing and pounding
Through the walls of our chests

I dreamed and knew
It would feel like this

Bent over the bed
Pushed hard against the wall
We straddle a chair
Mount the kitchen bench
I grip the shower screen
Kneel on the hallway floor

From behind
On the side
Me on top
We dive in
Again
And
Again

We hit the brink
Oblivion in reach
Ecstasy so near
We toy and play
Not wanting to arrive
Until we have
No more energy to give

We let go then,
There is no turning back
We cum once again

All I see is black

In a torrent of waves
That crash through my ears
Rush through my centre
Storm my groin
We pant in unison
Rapid breaths echo loud
Guttural groans sound out

We explode

You fill me
I drown you in return
Spent and elated
My head finds
The sweet hollow of your neck

We hold on tight
The pulsing subsides
In a gentle move
Out you slide
Pulling me close
You hug me hard
Cradle into my body
Kiss me good night

I return to my dream
Wishing you were here

And pray that
One day,
My dream
Will become real
And there you will be
Lying where you belong
Right here next to me.

A SECRET SHARED

We've cast aside the boundaries
We are in each other's space
I am both angel and your devil
Opening you to your deepness
Those long-held desires
You've told no one else
Are now a secret shared.

I will only hold you to
The pleasure that you seek
No hiding,
No lies
No limits
My mission is to be your finder
Your protector, promoter,
And guide.

Do you understand my motives,
Where this passion has laid its lines?
I've lost myself inside of you
In the labyrinth of your mind
My fears balance my excitement
For this adventure, we will take
You are about to find your calling
Gamble with your soul
Risk normality for ecstasy

Then finally,
Infinitely
Make you whole.

NOTHING TO FEAR

Let me play with your shadow side
You have nothing to fear from me
The darkness I see behind your smile
Excites me...
Entices me…

You've already proven what
a good man you are
But there is more of you
left to explore

Bind me
Blindfold my eyes
Tease my nipples
Bite my thighs

Bring me to the brink
Be a master to my slave
But don't expect submissiveness
Your attention makes me brave

You bring out my curiosity
Where limits don't exist
Take me home
Inside your darkness
Let me witness it

Whisper what you want
No request will be denied
I'm on this journey with you
I am here by your side

I assure you
It won't change a thing
About the way I feel

For all those desires,
Those callings you have...
I have had them too.

CREATURES OF THE NIGHT

Every time I think of you
A smile adorns my face
I think of all the things we'll do
Then my heart begins to race
There are so many secrets
That only as the best of friends we share
Freedom, fun and love bind us
And the depth with which we care
We are the shadow of one another
As much as we are the light
I lead you, you lead me
There is no wrong or right
I've known of you my whole life
But thought you were just a dream
It seems those nighttime picturescapes
Have led you straight to me
It's easy to imagine us

Running amok around the world
I may look like a librarian
But inside there is a gypsy girl
I look forward to our adventures
As creatures of the night
With you alongside of me
It will all work out just right

ONE OF THE BEAUTIFUL PEOPLE

I thought about you today
Just like I do every other day
I thought about how your life
Differed from mine
And the similarities we have
I always think of you
As one of the beautiful people
That all your friends are the same
You could easily grace
The pages of popular magazines
Toned and tanned
Flawless skin
Snow white teeth
In the 40s looking 30
In that way, I don't think
I could ever be the same
But I do match you, only
My beauty is on the inside
What I lack visually
I make up for in spirit
In kindness and generosity
In humour and love
Do you see that?
Or does external beauty counteract

Any shortfalls in a personality
Would you,
Do you,
Overlook selfishness,
Shallowness
Lack of depth of character
Because someone looks good
Standing beside you?
Do they,
Would they,
Ever take a slight step behind
To support you,
To put you first?
I hope that they would
Without question
Without resentment.
Not all the time
But enough of it,
To give you the balance
That you need.

ONE WORD

One word
And everything changes
One word
And the life we've dreamed of becomes real
One word
And all our desires are met
But fear binds us
The unknown looms large
What if it isn't what we expected?
What if?
What if,
It's better than we possibly could have imagined.
Do we stay
Complacent and stuck in the familiar,
Or do we grip hands
Leap together
And freefall into the unknown?
One word is all it takes
Yet one word could be any of many
Is it
Believe?
Faith?
Love?
Courage?
Or is it,
Could it possibly be

As simple
As just saying
YES!

I CAN'T NOT CARE

I could ask myself a thousand times
why does it matter,
why do I care so much,
yet the answer is always the same.
I can't not care.

When it's about you,
there is a whole world of possibility
in the palm of your hand.
I want to see where you go,
I want to cheer you on,
I want you to rest on me when weary,
celebrate all your wins,
and share the pain of your losses.

I can't not care,
when everything whispers to me,
that you are that piece of magic
that makes it all worthwhile.

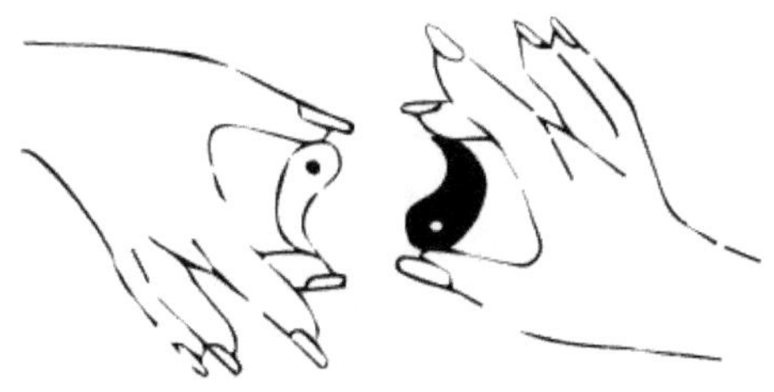

I can't not care,
when the key to your happiness,
also unlocks mine.

I can't not care,
when we are both the shadow
and light of the other.

I can't not care,
and feel any less deeply,
for our souls knew the other,
even before we met,
then they searched until we were found.

It is why I believe in all that you are,
not fearing your darkness,
basking in your light
and knowing you
without knowing you at all.

I can't not care,
because that would mean
my life has had no meaning.

FREE FALL INTO YOU

Somewhere between dusk and dawn
I go on a nightly adventure
To wherever you are
We explore new places
Find new lands
Discover each other

We are young and free
Without a care in the world
We are fearless and brave

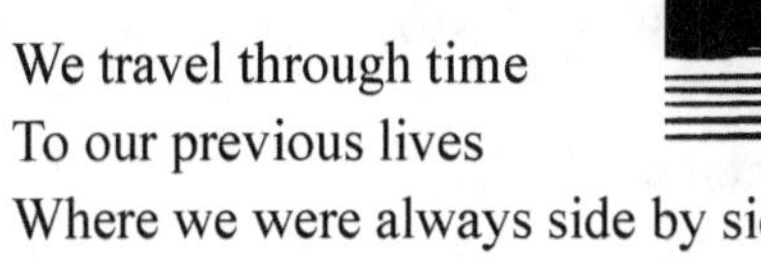

We travel through time
To our previous lives
Where we were always side by side

We make love often
With the hunger of teens
Every time feeling like the first

There's a newness and wonder
Curiosity abounds
All territories discovered, upturned

Both are eager to please
We learn through our senses
Practice hard at what the other has taught

Every crevice of your body
All the landscape of your skin
Has been committed to memory

Imprinted in my mind
Is your scent, your taste
The way you feel beneath my hands

Imprinted on my heart
Is who you are, what you stand for
How much I love you

Imprinted on my soul
Is both my mind and heart combined
And that you speak to it directly

Every waking moment
The invisible threads
Tug at me, reminding me

At night though,
At night...
I free fall into you

And trust that you are waiting
To catch me
With the open arms,
I know so well.

STRIPPED BARE

I lay before you stripped bare
Nothing to hide behind, no pretence
My words, little nuggets of gold
For stories to be told

If they reflect all that I feel
How much stronger is it in the real?
Can you see my playful side?
All the longing I can't hide.

Does my curiosity draw you in
To the imaginary life, we lead?
Every day is filled with wonder
Each moment, sacred thunder

That crashes down around us
Electrifies like a lightning strike
The days we share together
And the lust-filled, sex-fuelled nights

My imaginings are more like visions
Clear and very bold
Unsurpassed joy
To a life, we could possibly hold

If fear weren't a factor,
Would we take a leap of faith?
Deep down I know our union
Would make the Earth shake

Not because it's bad
In fact, it would be better than good
Some things are too hard to explain
And don't need to be understood.

What if knowing the devil was easy
But not like in the song
What if the devil
Was really us, deep down, all along

What if I knew your devil
And you knew mine as well
What if the place that they lived in
Was Heaven, and not actually hell?

Would we then embrace their spirit,
Set them both free,
To play amongst our angels
Like the children, they're meant to be

Is not wonder and curiosity,
The key to a life well lived?
Why do we need to dull them down
Force them into the underground?

What if the Heaven that we long for
Is ours if only we would reach for it?
Would we change the status quo,
Or fall back into a sleep,

Pretend it's only a dream
As we're not worthy in waking time,
To live a life of dreams come true
That seems to be gifted to only a special few.

If I have learnt anything
From my life up until now,
It is that the truth of you is everything
I have needed in my life

There is nothing we need to fear
Because what I feel is right
I accept the devil that is you
Embrace him with arms held wide

For he is the devil within me too
Let's let them play,
Live life our way
Together, side by side.

MORE

You have known women who are beautiful
I wonder how I compare
Am I too much or not enough,
Should I really care?

Do they know You as I do?
Want only the very best for You?
Do they reach into the place,
Where the true You,
The real You
Likes to hide?

Do they know your fears,
Or your capacity to care?
Do they see beyond the shell,
To the naked pearl that's hidden deep inside?

Do they listen to your dreams?
Encourage You to reach them?
Believe in You more than themselves?
Do they know what turns You on,
Or where your thoughts go when alone?
Do they love You all night long,
Or only when it suits them?

Is it okay to ask these things,
When I am just watching from the wings?
Knowing that,
I know You more
Appreciate You more
Respect You more,
Than any of them combined.
So maybe I am not good enough
Or beautiful enough,
Or nothing to you at all,
But there is one thing that I am certain of,
As it is my soul,
That spoke to me.
It's the purest form of all I am,
The one You know so well.

There is no one else in this lifetime, the next,
Or even the one before
That will ever feel the way I feel
And need You
Want You
Or
Unconditionally Love
You
More.

FORGIVE

Forgive me for loving you and
wishing you were mine
Forgive me for caring too much
crossing the friendship line
Forgive me for knowing you
probably better than you know yourself
Forgive me for seeing past all the layers,
to the real person inside
Forgive me for wanting the very best for you,
encouraging you to shine.

Forgive yourself for being the man
that all men should be
Forgive yourself for being afraid
to have all your desires met
Forgive yourself for thinking,
you don't deserve the best
Forgive yourself for always putting,
the needs of others first
Forgive yourself for not believing in
the things that you deserve

Forgiveness is one of those things
that is more than merely a word
Forgiveness is the only thing
that can set you free in this world
I forgive you, for being the best
of all the people I have known
I forgive me,
for wanting a little piece of you
to call my own
I forgive us, for being, the flip side of the other,
for fighting over little things in order to cover
a power that is bigger and beyond us both
It's the one thing often misunderstood
that brought you to me
It's the mystery of this wonderful world,
it was our destiny.

SOULS COLLIDE

The house is so quiet
As I lay in bed alone
With only my thoughts
To keep me company.

There is so much love
In this home
Yet when I think of you
I know there is so much more
It's an adventure waiting to happen.

How can it be,
I thought I was settled
Then you came along
Turned my world upside down
Woke me from a slumber
I never knew I was in.

You made me feel alive
Made me a better person
Cracked my heart wide open
So that love for everything
Came pouring out.

This is what happens
When souls collide and

Flames ignite
When trust, love, and friendship bind
Cementing an unconditional acceptance
Of each other.

I go on each day
As if you are just a ghost
You over there, me here
A distance that is short
Yet wider than an ocean.

You are no ghost though
You are the truest thing
I have ever known.
In this crazy life,
We live

I feel you every second
Think of you more often
Dream about you always
Wish you understood
I hope you know it too

That I am your missing piece
The key that opens up
The door
To a life fulfilled in every way

Just as you are mine
But it isn't our time yet
We still have lessons to learn
So, I wait patiently
Live with the choices we make
Knowing that one day
In this life or the next
We will rule the world together.

INSIDE YOUR HEART

There are times I know exactly what you think
And others, I don't have a clue
In my twisted fantasy world
I am always beside you
I wish you'd say the words to me
I often long to hear
My fragile mind can only stand so much
As it is always filled with fear
That one day, you'll see beyond my words
And not like what appears
For beauty is only inside of me
And not the physical sphere
I can lie to myself and ease the pain
And say it doesn't matter
It works for just a little bit
To quiet the mind chatter
We have parallel lives
With wants and needs
Crossing over only in my dreams
I walk beside you
But so far apart
I want only to live
Inside your heart.

GYPSY QUEEN

To be a gypsy
Wild and free
That is the life
I'd choose for me
No ties or bonds
No hurts or cons
I could come and go
As I please.

I'd roam the world
With total ease
Let only in those
Who feel the same as me,
My love would be hidden
But my time would be free.

No one could hurt me
Although judge as they might
There'd be no angry words
Or begging to fight.
My only companions
Are nature's best
The winds and the sun,
Trees, flowers in bloom,
A waterfall to bathe in,
By the light of the moon.

I'd leave little a footprint
In this world's beautiful room.

But would I be lonely,
Feel afraid or lost?
Would I covet love,
Long to belong,
Or would I live a solitary
Life all along?

Would I still dream of you,
See your name written in the stars?
Have memories yet to live,
Knowing you are out there too,
Would I roam the world
Just looking for you?

I know you're there,
I feel it in my bones.
My blood runs hot
When I whisper your name.
I have this feeling
You feel the same.

Would we know each other
At first glance?
Would we intimately know
The lovers' dance?
Would my heart skip a beat,

When our eyes first meet?
Will my soul know you,
Welcome you home.

Everything tells me
This is how it would be
When I finally find you,
Or you find me.
Together we'd roam
From one end of the world
To the other,
The Gypsy Queen
And her Gypsy King lover.

THE MIRROR NEVER LIES

In you I found myself
Or at least the version
I wanted to be

I never knew that
Half of me lived
Inside someone else

So I'd spent my life searching
Missing something
Without a name

Then you appeared
I sensed instinctively
That my puzzle had been solved

I could read your thoughts
Feel your emotions
As if they were mine too

Where once there was dark
Only light shone
My withered soul began to bloom

The chains that tethered me
Slowly loosened
Releasing me from my inner shackles

I stood before you
Broken and bruised
Raw, unworthy, unknown

Your smile thawed my frozen heart
Your eyes saw deep into me
And I reflected You back

It was then that I understood
What unconditional love and acceptance meant
I learnt to trust for real

I am no longer afraid
You showed me my courage
I will always look to you for the answers

You are my mirror
Just as I am yours
Reflecting the truth of who we are

For the mirror never lies

MOSAIC HEART

My heart is a mosaic
Made up of shattered pieces,
Glued and gilded together
With the gold of life.

Each piece is a person,
Loved and lost.
Each crack a wound,
That tells the story
Of places and people
That left their mark
Upon my heart.

It still beats strong,
This heart of mine.
My blood, made of love,
Floods my body with hope,
My mind, with faith,
That all the sorrow
And the pain
Is only surface deep.

That joy and love,
Laughter and longing
Seep from deep inside,
Glaze the heart's surface

Sealing memories and feelings
Protecting them forever,
So as to remind me ...

What forgiveness is
That wounds heal
Sorrow fades
And love in all its glory,
Grows when shared,
Strengthens when mirrored
Heals everything, always.

My mosaic heart may have splintered,
Been wounded,
More times than I can count.
But I,
I will never be broken.